PRAISE MY PET

ADULT COLORING BOOK

Color Artie!

Color Gabby!

3

Color Sweetie!

Color
Rusty and Sargent!

Color Biscuit!

Color Cloud!

Color
Missy and Tia!

6

Color
Ozzie and TC!

8

Color Bella!

Color Porsche!

Color
Freddo and Tucker!

9

Color
Gabriel and Arabella!

Color Jasmine!

10

Color
Preston and Baxter!

Color
Teddy Bear!

11

Color
Fleanne, Ticky Lee, Cricket and Beetle Bailey!

12

Color Leila!

Color
Bella and Nellie!

13

Color
Maxine, Shadow and Saydie!

15

Color Sophie and Izzy!

Color Brownie!

Color
Molly, Marshmallow and Bear!

Color Storm!

17

Color Pointdexter!

Color
Paris and Halo!

19

Color Riley!

Color Hank!

Color Cash!

22

Color Kyah!

Color
Ubu and Twitch!

23

Color
Blessing, Christian and Bubby!

24

Color
Lil Man, Bear and Champ!

27

Color
Atlas and Jethro!

Color
Power and Pixie!

28

Color Han Solo!

Color Jasmine and Cooper!

29

Color B B!

Color
Theodore Bear and Maximilian!

Color Zena!

Color
Maltese and Itzo!

31

Color Mollie Mae!

Color
Mozzi and Kisses!

32

Color Jack!

Color Mocha!

Color Dakoda!

33

Color
Tobias, Jacob and Boots!

Color Lady!

35

Color
Milo, Chase and Nina!

36

Color Luger!

Color Tazzy Bouchea!

37

Color
Bowzer, Sandy,
Beau and Smokey!

38

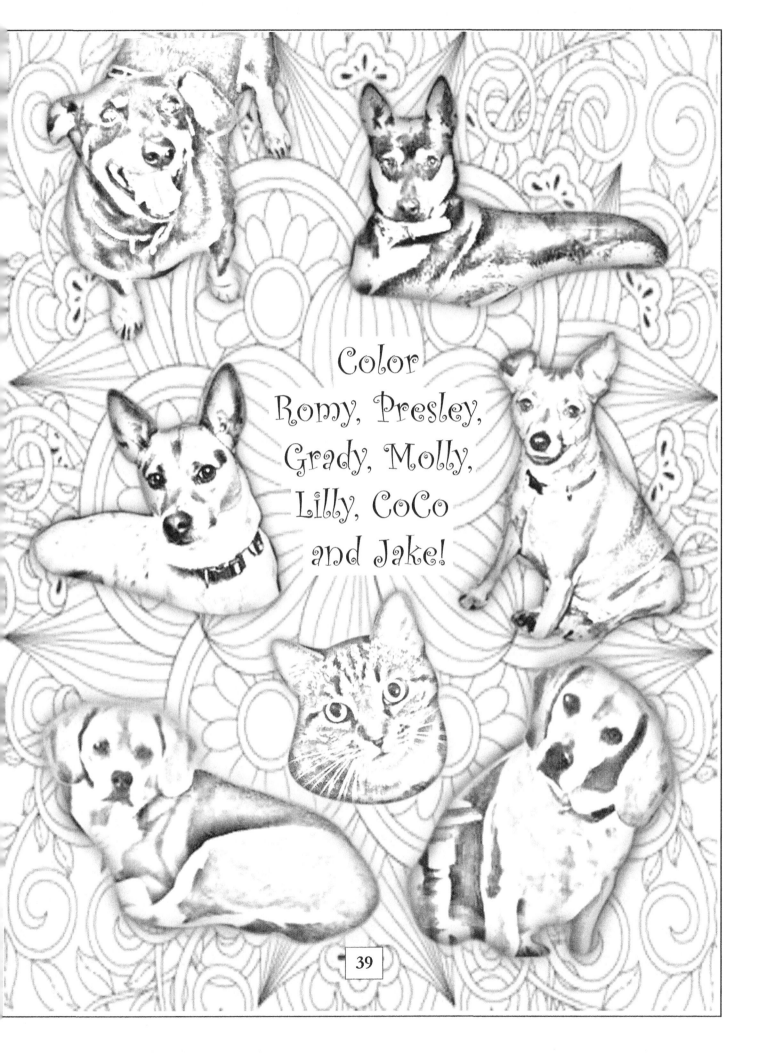

Color
Romy, Presley,
Grady, Molly,
Lilly, CoCo
and Jake!

Color Einstein!

Color Aurora and Buddy!

Color Frank!

40

Color Sheeba!

41

Color Bella!

Color
Ky, Mandy and Maggie!

43

Color Rosie!

Color
Buddy and Princie!

44

Color Peanut!

45

Color
Chloe and Cooper!

Color Memphis!

Color Scarlet!

46

47

Color Kangee!

Color
Koal and Chubby!

48

Color Osito!

Color
Jemma and Timone!

49

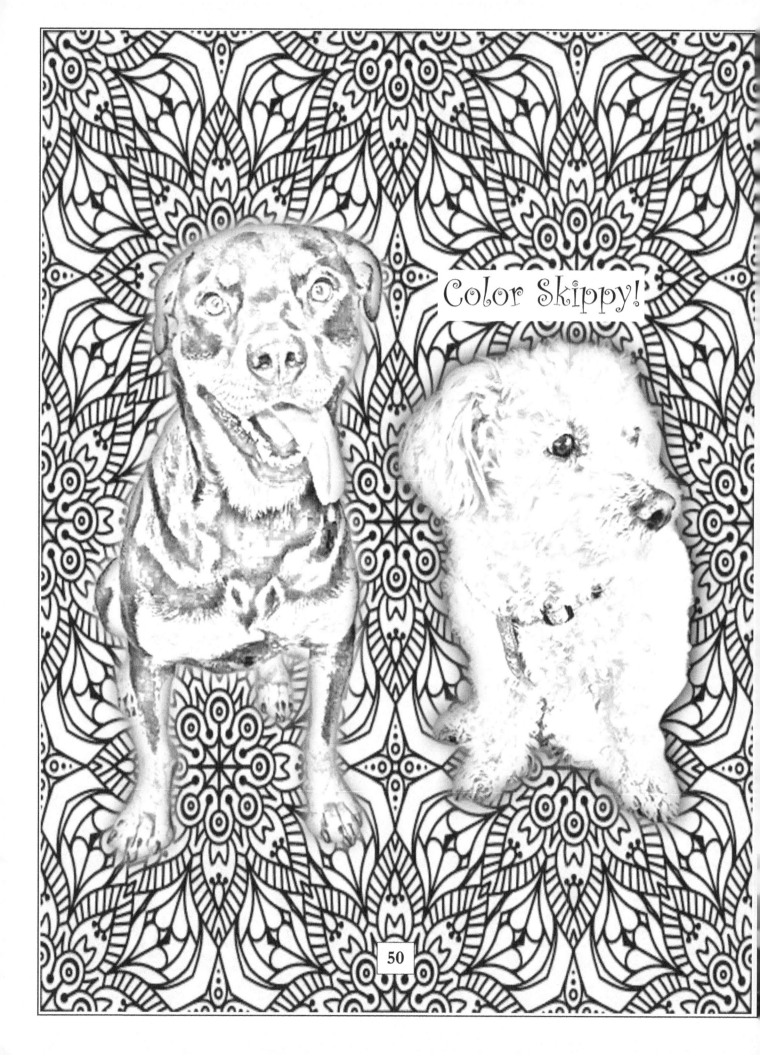

Color Skippy!

51

Color
Ponder and Whiskey!

52

Color
Curious George and Opie!

Color Colbie!

54

Color Pluto!

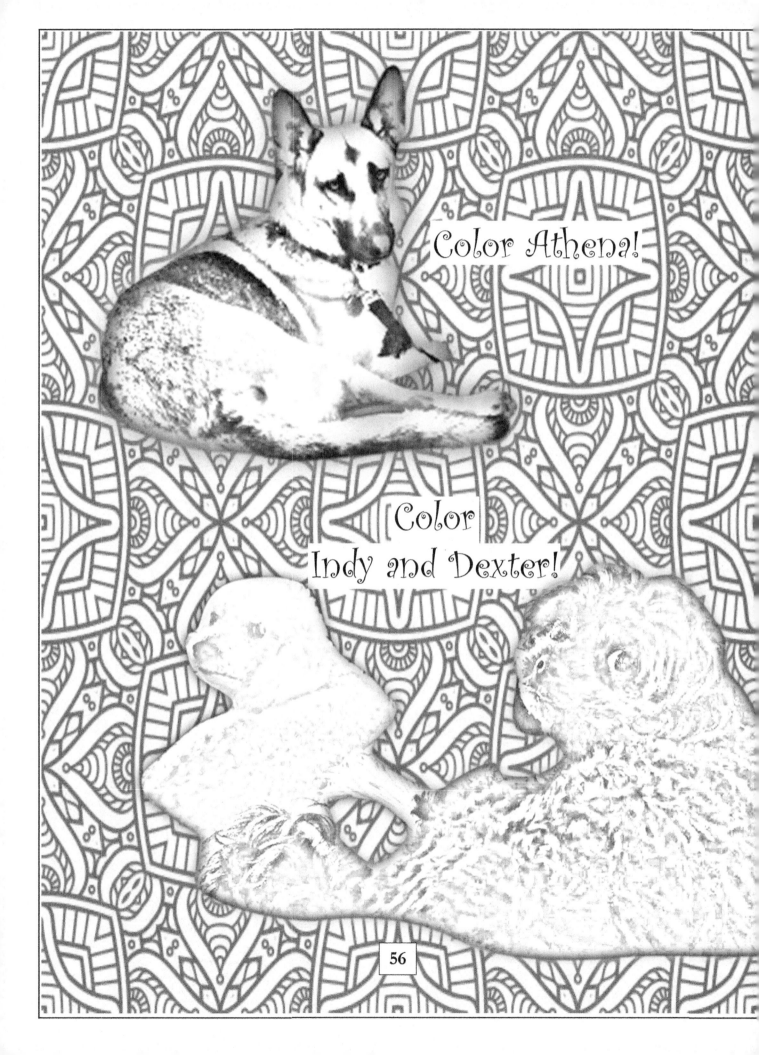

Color Athena!

Color
Indy and Dexter!

56

Color
Killer and Zoey!

Color
Candie Cutie Broyles!

Color
Sassy and Fannie Mae!

59

Color
Benji and Harley!

60

Color Aspen!

61

Color Dexter!

Color Milo!

Color
Yorkies Ollie, TT, Olliver and Autumn!

63

Color
Bentleigh and Rugar!

Color Chester!

64

Color
Smokey, Pepperoni, Lady and Angel!

Color
Maleficent JoeC and
Maleficent's Prince Leon!

Color Jinxy Westby!

Color Teddy!

Color Lexi!

67

Color
Butch, Baby and Buster!

Color
Lil. Mam and Mammies!

Color Penny!

70

Color Pancho!

Color Kenai!

72

Color Beyonce'!

73

Color Hyundai!

74

Color Oscar!

75

Color
Sir Charles Barkley!

76

Color
Rowdy Ray Reno!

77

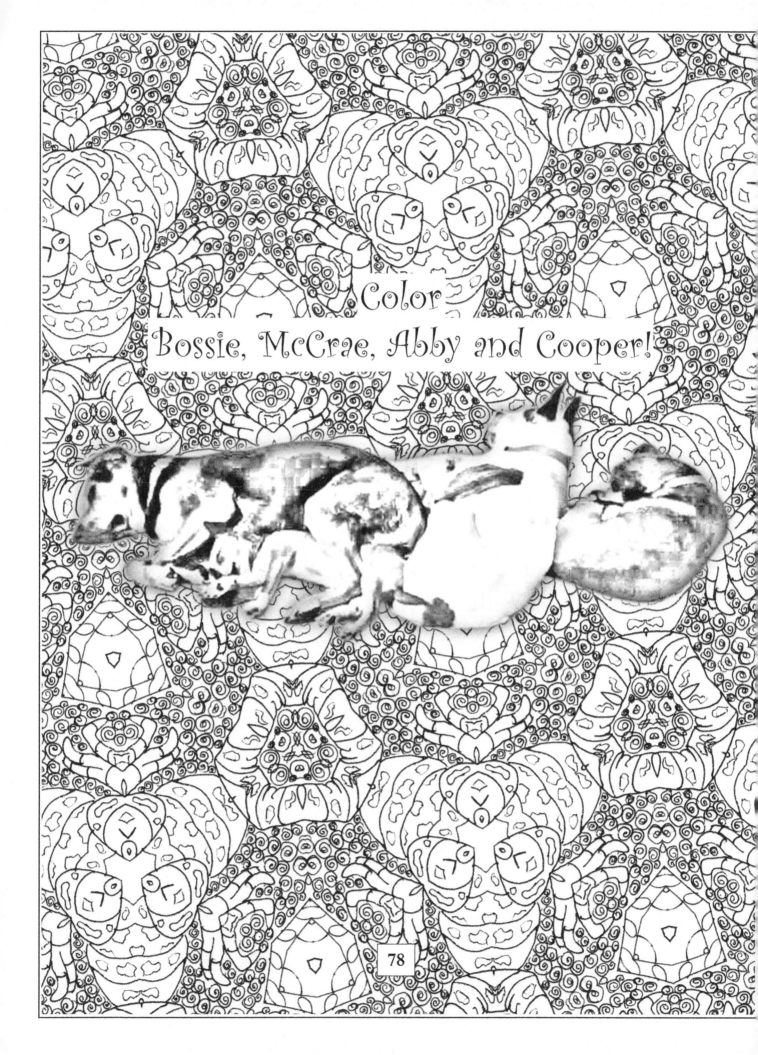

Color
Bossie, McCrae, Abby and Cooper!

78

Color
Beau and Bella!

Color Blue!

79

Color Pugsy!

Color GiGi Cannoli!

80

Color
Shasta, Dylan and Honey!

81

Color Elvis!

Color
Baby Chewy and Scout!

82

Color
Cirrus and River!

83

Color Angel!

Color Baby!

84

Color Daisy May!

Color
Boo and Oliver!

85

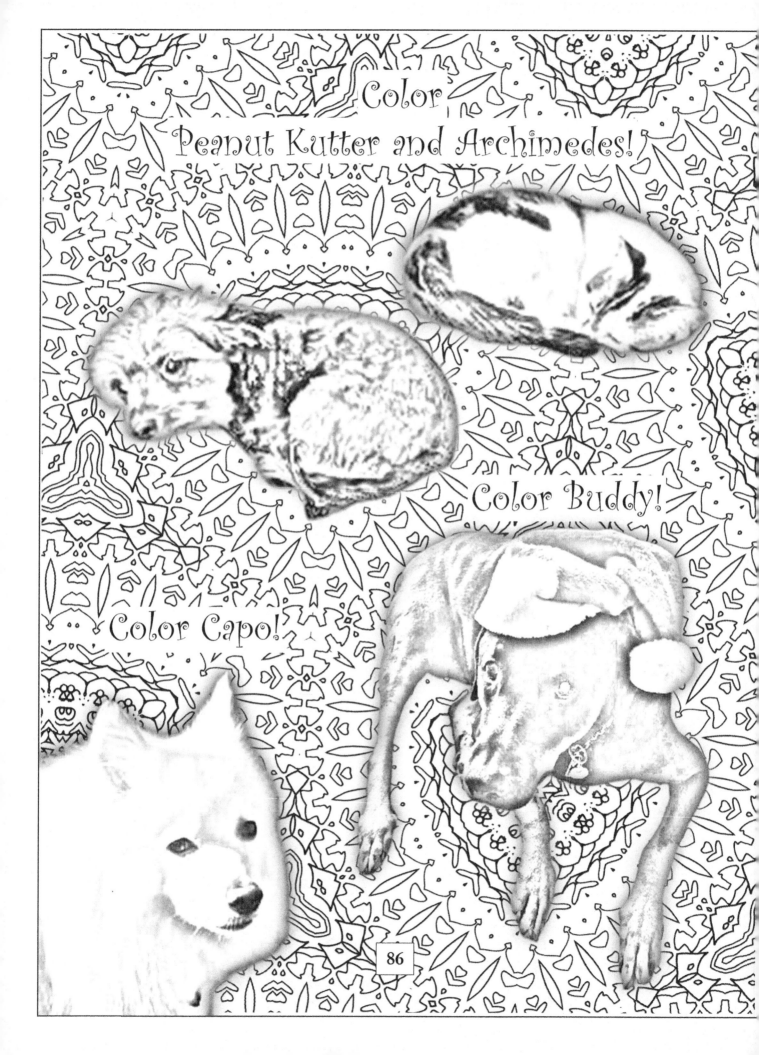

Color
Peanut Kutter and Archimedes!

Color Buddy!

Color Capo!

86

Color Riggs!

Color Bella!

Color
Moto and Emma-lee!

Color
Ozzie and Tobie!

Color Charlie!

Color Scout!

88

Color
Jak and Georgia!

Color Winston!

Color Molly!

90

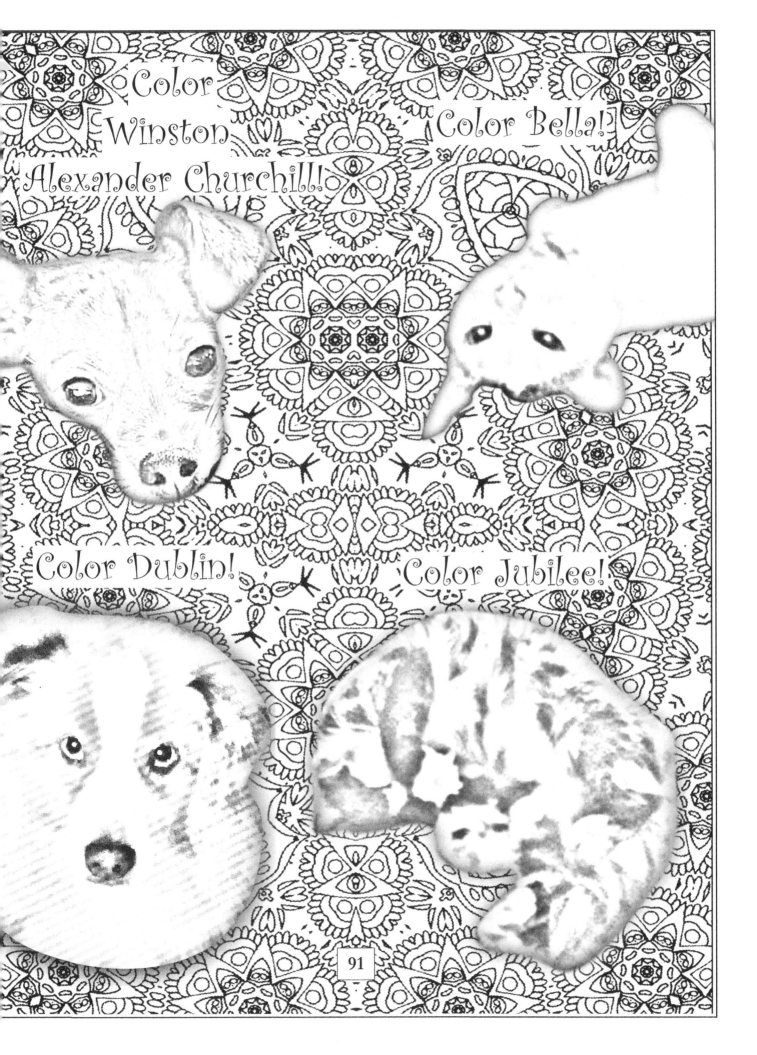

Color
Winston
Alexander Churchill!

Color Bella!

Color Dublin!

Color Jubilee!

91

Color
Daisy Mae!

92

Color
Sookie, Rip and Heidi!

93

Color Eko!

Color
Tara and Bailey!

94

Color Bear!

Color
Rue and Waffles!

95

Color
Lilly and Daisy!

Color Phobe!

96

Color Zoie!

Color Sven!

97

Color Sadie!

Color Zander and Noah!

98

Color
Tabatha, Mika, Sally and Cooper Doo!

99

Color Bacardi!

Color
Bailey and Keela!

100

Color
Batman, Bootsie and Tootsie!

Color
Jaxon and Oliver!

Color Mochi!

102

We hope you enjoyed our coloring book! If you'd like to see YOUR pet in one of our upcoming coloring books, visit www.praisemypet.com/pages/send-us-your-pet-photos

Happy coloring!

Made in the USA
Monee, IL
05 February 2023

27187192R00057